Bible Question Class Books

Bible Study Questions on
Ephesians and Philippians
by David E. Pratte

A workbook suitable for Bible classes,
family studies, or personal Bible study

Available in print at
www.gospelway.com/sales

Bible Study Questions on Ephesians and Philippians:
A workbook suitable for Bible classes, family studies,
or personal Bible study

ISBN-13: 978-1517253127
ISBN-10: 1517253128

Printed books, booklets, and tracts available at
www.gospelway.com/sales
Free Bible study articles online at
www.gospelway.com
Free Bible courses online at
www.biblestudylessons.com
Free class books at
www.biblestudylessons.com/classbooks
Free commentaries on Bible books at
www.biblestudylessons.com/commentary
Contact the author at
www.gospelway.com/comments

Note carefully: No teaching in any of our materials is intended or should ever be construed to justify or to in any way incite or encourage personal vengeance or physical violence against any person.

"He who glories, let him glory in the Lord"
– 1 Corinthians 1:31

Front Page Photo

The Theater in Ephesus

"So the whole city was filled with confusion, and rushed into the theater with one accord, having seized Gaius and Aristarchus, Macedonians, Paul's travel companions. And when Paul wanted to go in to the people, the disciples would not allow him. Then some of the officials of Asia, who were his friends, sent to him pleading that he would not venture into the theater."
Acts 19:29-31 (NKJV)

Other Books by the Author

Topical Bible Studies

Growing a Godly Marriage & Raising Godly Children
Why Believe in God, Jesus, and the Bible? (evidences)
The God of the Bible (study of the Father, Son, and Holy Spirit)
Grace, Faith, and Obedience: The Gospel or Calvinism?
Kingdom of Christ: Future Millennium or Present Spiritual Reign?
Do Not Sin Against the Child: Abortion, Unborn Life, & the Bible
True Words of God: Bible Inspiration and Preservation

Commentaries on Bible Books

Genesis	*Gospel of Mark*
Joshua and Ruth	*Gospel of John*
Judges	*Acts*
1 Samuel	*Romans*
Ezra, Nehemiah, and Esther	*Ephesians*
Job	*Philippians and Colossians*
Proverbs	*Hebrews*
	1 & 2 Peter

Bible Question Class Books

Genesis	*Gospel of John*
Joshua and Ruth	*Acts*
Judges	*Romans*
1 Samuel	*1 Corinthians*
Ezra, Nehemiah, and Esther	*2 Corinthians and Galatians*
Job	*Ephesians and Philippians*
Proverbs	*Colossians, 1&2 Thessalonians*
Ecclesiastes	*1 & 2 Timothy, Titus, Philemon*
Isaiah	*Hebrews*
Gospel of Matthew	*General Epistles (James - Jude)*
Gospel of Mark	*Revelation*
Gospel of Luke	

Workbooks with Study Notes

Jesus Is Lord: Workbook on the Fundamentals of the Gospel of Christ
Following Jesus: Workbook on Discipleship
God's Eternal Purpose in Christ: Workbook on the Theme of the Bible

Visit our website at <u>www.gospelway.com/sales</u> to see a current list of books in print.

Bible Study Questions on Ephesians and Philippians

Introduction:

This workbook was designed for Bible class study, family study, or personal study. The class book is suitable for teens and up. The questions contain minimal human commentary, but instead urge students to study to understand Scripture.

Enough questions are included for teachers to assign as many questions as they want for each study session. Studies may proceed at whatever speed and depth will best accomplish the needs of the students.

Questions labeled "think" are intended to encourage students to apply what they have learned. When questions refer to a map, students should consult maps in a Bible dictionary or similar reference work or in the back of their Bibles. (Note: My abbreviation "*b/c/v*" means "book, chapter, and verse.")

For class instruction, I urge teachers to assign the questions as homework so students come to class prepared. Then let class time consist of *discussion* that focuses on the Scriptures themselves. Let the teacher use other Scriptures, questions, applications, and comments to promote productive discussion, not just reading the questions to see whether they were answered "correctly." Please, do *not* let the class period consist primarily of the following: "Joe, will you answer number 1?" "Sue, what about number 2?" Etc.

I also urge students to emphasize the *Bible* teaching. Please, do not become bogged down over "What did the author mean by question #5?" My meaning is relatively unimportant. The issue is what the Bible says. Concentrate on the meaning and applications of Scripture. If a question helps promote Bible understanding, stay with it. If it becomes unproductive, move on.

The questions are not intended just to help students understand the Scriptures. They are also designed to help students learn good principles of Bible study. Good Bible study requires defining the meaning of keywords, studying parallel passages, explaining the meaning of the text clearly, making applications, and defending the truth as well as exposing religious error. I have included questions to encourage students to practice all these study principles.

Note that some questions on this book are more difficult and advanced. The study leader may want to skip some questions if he/she is teaching a less advanced study.

Finally, I encourage plain applications of the principles studied. God's word is written so souls may please God and have eternal life. Please study it with the respect and devotion it deserves!

For whatever good this material achieves, to God be the glory.

Bible study commentary and notes to accompany some of our workbooks are available at www.gospelway.com/sales

© David E. Pratte, June 23, 2017

Assignments on Ephesians 1

Please read the whole book of Ephesians at least once as we study chapter 1. Answer the following questions on chap. 1

1. Who wrote this letter, and to whom is it addressed – 1:1?

2. List some things you know about the author.

---

3. **Special Assignment:** Study a Bible dictionary or similar book about the city of Ephesus. List some things you learned.

---

4. Make a list of Bible **passages** outside the book of Ephesians that refer to the city or church at Ephesus (use a concordance and cross-references).

5. Summarize what the Bible says about Ephesus (the city or the church) outside the book of Ephesians.

6. After you have read the whole epistle, state the theme of the book.

7. List some of the main points discussed in each chapter.

8. What position did Paul claim to have, and who gave it to him – 1:1?

9. Summarize the Bible teaching about apostles. What work did they do? What qualifications did they have, etc.?

10. What evidence is there elsewhere that Paul was an apostle?

Bonus assignment: As we study the book of Ephesians, make a list of the verses that refer to the church and summarize what they teach.

---

11. What is a saint? Proof? How does the Bible teaching about saints compare to the concept many people have of a saint?

12. What blessings did Paul seek on the Ephesians' behalf – 1:2,3?

13. Who is the source of spiritual blessings? Where are they found? (Think: In what different ways is the word "bless" used in 1:3?)

14. **Define** "spiritual." List some examples of spiritual blessings. (Think: Study the expression "in heavenly places" as used in Ephesians. What does it mean?)

---

15. **Special Assignment:** What does it mean to be "in Christ," and how does one come into Christ (see John 17:20-23; 2 Cor. 5:17; Rom. 6:3,4; Gal. 3:26,27; see cross-references)?

---

16. **Define** "election" (or "chose") and "predestine."

17. Note 1:5,9,11. According to what standard does God choose or predestine people? On what basis does He decide? (Think: Where can we go to learn about His will or purpose?)

18. "In whom" are we chosen –1:4,5? Review what we studied about this idea. What conclusions can you reach about whether we have a choice in this election?

19. List **passages** elsewhere showing how many people God wants saved or how many He has made salvation available to.

20. List **passages** elsewhere showing salvation is conditional and man has the power to choose to obey or not.

21. According to 1:4,5, what is the goal or result of our election?

22. **Case Study:** Calvinism says that election or predestination means, before the world began, God unconditionally chose certain individuals to be saved, regardless of their character, will, or choice. Others He chose to be lost. According to what we have studied, how would you respond? Explain Biblical election and predestination as well as you can.

23. What is the purpose of our predestination according to 1:6? (Think: If we truly strive to realize this purpose, how will we act?)

24. In whom are we accepted? To whom does this refer? Proof?

25. **Define** "redemption" and "grace."

26. What blessings are found in Christ according to 1:7? (Think: How do we receive the benefits of Jesus' blood?)

Workbook on Ephesians and Philippians

27. **Special Assignment:** Prepare a short report on the significance of blood in the Bible, especially as regards forgiveness. Why did blood need to be shed for remission?

28. List other verses about grace. Why do we need it?

29. **Define** "mystery" as used in Ephesians – 1:9. List several verses where it is used.

30. Should the gospel be considered such a mystery today that we cannot understand it? Explain.

31. Whose pleasure and purpose are being accomplished in God's plan for redemption? Where can we learn about that will?

32. **Define** "dispensation" – 1:10. Is this a time period? In what sense does it relate to the fullness of time?

33. What did God intend to do in this dispensation? What things will be affected? (Think: Explain how this happened.)

34. What is provided in Christ according to 1:11?

35. We are predestined according to what (1:11; compare verses 5,9)?

36. What is the purpose of our predestination (1:12)? Where else has this been stated? (Think: Who is the "we" of verse 12 and the "you" of verse 13? Compare 2:11-16.)

37. **Special Assignment:** What has to happen before people can believe – 1:13? Explain the role that the gospel has in our salvation.

38. **Define** "seal" and "guarantee" (or "earnest") – 1:13,14.

39. What other **passages** speak of the Holy Spirit as a seal or guarantee? (Think: In what sense is the Holy Spirit an earnest or seal?)

40. Does this seal or guarantee prove we cannot be lost? Explain. (Think: In what sense is the Holy Spirit a guarantee "till the redemption of the purchased possession"?)

41. What characteristics did the Ephesians possess according to 1:15? Why are these characteristics important?

42. What did Paul do for them – 1:16?

43. List other verses regarding Christians praying for one another. Explain why this practice is important.

44. List six things Paul prayed for on behalf of the Ephesians – 1:17-19.

45. **Define** "wisdom," "revelation," and "enlightenment" – 1:17,18. (Think: How does wisdom differ from knowledge?)

---

46. **Special Assignment:** How does one obtain wisdom and enlightenment (see James 1:3-8; Heb. 5:14; 2 Tim. 3:15-17)? (Think: Must God send direct revelation to answer a prayer for these blessings? Explain.)

---

47. What is the Christian's hope (give b/c/v)? (Think: How are we called to this hope?)

48. What is our inheritance (give b/c/v)? (Think: In what sense are there "riches of glory" in this inheritance?)

49. Whose power benefits us – 1:19,20?

50. How has God already demonstrated His power? (Think: If God raised Jesus, what does this prove regarding His power toward us?)

51. Where did God place Jesus – 1:20,21?

52. **Special Assignment:** Study the significance of God's right hand. List other **passages**. What is Jesus doing there?

53. What is Jesus over – 1:21? Study the significance of these terms.

54. What does this tell you about Jesus? (Think: Could this be true if Jesus is not Deity? Explain.)

55. What position does Jesus have according to 1:22,23? Explain the illustration.

56. Over how many things is Jesus Head to the church? Where is Jesus now (verse 20)?

57. **Case Study:** Modern denominations have a man or group of men who serve as "head" of the denomination or who make laws for the church. What application does 1:22,23 have regarding this practice?

58. **Case Study:** Some people claim that all the denominations are pleasing to God. How many bodies can one head have? Explain the application to denominations.

59. **Define** "fullness." In what sense does Jesus fill all in all? In what sense is the church the fullness of Christ?

Assignments on Ephesians 2

Please read the whole book of Ephesians again as we study chapter 2. Answer the following questions on chap. 2.

1. **Define** "dead" and "alive" as used in 2:1. Is this physical death? Proof? What causes this death?

2. List other **passages** regarding this kind of life and death. What lessons can we learn from the expressions "dead" and "alive" (compare 2:11-13)?

3. How is a sinful life described in 2:2,3? (Think: Who is the "prince of the power of the air"?)

4. **Case Study:** Some people say we are born guilty of Adam's sin and inherit a sin nature from him, so we cannot do right. How would you respond? What made these people sinners?

5. In what sense are people "by nature" children of wrath? (Note: Whose sins caused the conditions described in context?) (Think: How is the word "walk" used here?)

6. What has God done for people dead in sin – 2:4,5?

7. In light of 2:1-3, in what sense are we "made alive"? List other **passages** about this.

8. What motivated God to do this?

9. How is being made alive described in 2:6? Where else is this concept discussed? (Think: In what sense do we sit together in heavenly places in Christ?)

10. What does this show – 2:7? (Think: To whom is this shown and when?)

11. How are we saved, and how are we not saved – 2:8,9?

12. Make a list of **passages** showing faith is essential to salvation. (Think: Do any of these passages say that obedience or baptism is not needed for salvation?)

13. Make a list of **passages** showing whether or not obedience or works are essential to salvation.

14. Compare Ephesians 2:4-9 to Colossians 2:12,13. Make a list of similarities. Based on this, does Ephesians 2:8,9 prove baptism is not essential to salvation? Explain.

15. **Special Assignment:** In light of the above information, explain how salvation is a gift of God, not of works.

16. What does 2:10 teach about works?

17. Who are the circumcision and the uncircumcision? Which one is addressed in 2:11? (Think: What is the significance of these terms?)

18. Describe their condition according to 2:12. (Think: What caused these conditions? How does this relate to 2:1,5?)

19. Give other Scriptures about these conditions.

20. **Define** "commonwealth." What "promise" is referred to here?

21. What did Jesus do regarding the Gentiles' problems – 2:13? How? Explain.

22. What barrier separated Jew and Gentile – 2:14,15? (Think: Explain how and why this was a wall of separation.)

23. What did Jesus do about this? How? What condition resulted? (Think: What can we learn about relations between people of different backgrounds in the church?)

24. List other **passages** about the removal of the Old Testament.

25. What did Jesus do according to 2:16? **Define** "reconcile." (Think: Explain the connection between reconciliation to God and reconciliation between people.)

26. Where are we reconciled? What is the "body"? By what means are we reconciled? (Think: How many bodies are there? What application can be made to denominations?)

27. **Case Study:** Some people say the 10 Commands are still in effect. Others say Jews will again have special privileges in the millennium. Explain the application of verses 14-16.

28. Who are those who are near and those who are far – 2:17? What did Christ do for them both?

29. What do we receive through Jesus – 2:18? How does this differ from previous conditions (verse 12)? (Think: What does the Holy Spirit have to do with this?)

30. List other **passages** showing we can come to God or reach Him through Jesus.

31. Explain the contrast made in 2:19.

32. What are we citizens of? What household are we members of? Give other b/c/v to prove your answer. (Think: If we are already citizens, then does the kingdom exist? What application can be made to those who claim the kingdom will not begin till Jesus returns?)

33. What role did the cornerstone have in ancient buildings?

34. List other **passages** regarding the foundation of the church and/or Jesus as chief cornerstone.

35. **Case Study:** Some churches teach that the church is built on the Peter as the foundation. Based on the above verses, who is the true foundation of the church? Explain.

36. **Special Assignment:** Explain the sense in which this is the foundation "of" the apostles and prophets? Does the passage say they **are** the foundation? Does this require apostles and prophets or their successors to be living on earth? (Hint: Is Christ the cornerstone living on earth? Note Luke 16:29-31.)

37. Into what does the building grow – 2:21 – i.e., what kind of building is formed? (Think: How does this happen? Compare 1 Peter 2:4-8.)

38. List other **passages** discussing us as God's temple or showing God dwells in us.

39. Based on the above verses, explain the sense in which we are a temple or habitation of God.

Workbook on Ephesians and Philippians

Assignments on Ephesians 3

Please read the whole book of Ephesians again as we study chapter 3. Answer the following questions on chap. 3.

1. Read 3:1 and 3:14. Read the context and explain the connection between these verses.

2. How did Paul describe himself – 3:1? What does this tell about his circumstances?

3. What grace had Paul received – 3:2? (Think: Explain "dispensation." Cf. 1:10.)

4. What did this have to do with Gentiles? List other **passages** about Paul's special responsibility to Gentiles.

5. **Define** "mystery" – 3:3-5. Where else is it mentioned in Ephesians and elsewhere?

6. **Define** "revelation." Who revealed the mystery, and to whom was it revealed?

7. When was the mystery unknown? Is it still unknown? Explain.

8. What did Paul do with his knowledge of the mystery? Why? (Think: When and where did Paul write briefly about this before?)

9. **Application**: What lesson can we learn regarding whether or not Scripture can be understood? List other **passages** showing we can understand God's will.

10. What can we learn regarding Scripture and how we learn God's will? Must we be directly inspired to know God's will? Explain. (Think: What other passages teach these ideas?)

11. What did the mystery (3:3-5) reveal regarding the Gentiles – 3:6? How did this differ from their previous status (chapter 2)? (Think: Did the Old Testament reveal anything regarding God's blessing for Gentiles? Explain.)

12. What role did Paul have in these blessings to Gentiles – 3:7? **Define** "minister." (Think: What is meant by "effective working of his power.")

13. How did Paul describe his position compared to other saints – 3:8? What other **passages** are similar? (Think: Why did Paul so view himself?)

14. Yet what was Paul permitted to do? In what sense was this grace? (Think: How are these "unsearchable riches"?)

15. How long was the mystery hidden – 3:9? Who hid it? Is it still hidden? (Cf. vv 3-5.)

16. **Define** "manifold." Through what is God's wisdom made known – 3:10?

17. To whom is this wisdom made known? (Think: How does the church make known God's wisdom?)

18. All this works according to what – 3:11? Where else have we read of this purpose?

19. **Application**: Explain the application of 3:10,11 to the following:
* Premillennialists who say Jesus came to establish the kingdom but changed His mind and established the church instead.

* Denominationalists who say the church is not essential to salvation.

* People who add to or take from God's pattern for the church.

Workbook on Ephesians and Philippians

20. What blessings do we have according to 3:12? Why are these important?

21. What concern does Paul express in 3:13? (Think: Considering Paul's circumstances, why might he express such a concern?)

22. To whom did Paul bow – 3:14? What does it mean for the family to be named after Him (3:15)? (Think: To whom did Paul address his prayer?)

23. Note the word "that" repeated in 3:16-19. List 4 things "that" Paul prayed for.

24. What strength does God provide, and what are some ways He provides it?

25. What does it mean for Christ to dwell in us (give other b/c/v)? How does He do it?

26. *Application*: Explain the sense in which love roots and grounds us – 3: 17.

27. What do we need to know – 3:18,19? How can we know it if it passes knowledge? (Think: What does Paul mean by "width, length, depth, and height"?)

28. What may we be filled with? What does this mean?

29. What can God do – 3:20? How?

30. What should God receive for all He has done – 3:21? For how long? (Think: Would this be so if the church was not essential to salvation or was an unplanned change in God's plan?)

Assignments on Ephesians 4

Please read the whole book of Ephesians again as we study chapter 4. Answer the following questions on chap. 4.

1. What did Paul challenge the Ephesians to do in 4:1? Explain how this is done.

---

2. **Special Assignment: Define** each of the following keywords in 4:2. Then for each one, explain why it is important to unity and peace in the church.

Lowliness

Gentleness or meekness

Longsuffering

Bearing with one another in love

3. What should we be diligent to keep according to 4:3? Explain what role the Holy Spirit has in God's plan for our unity and peace (hint: consider the context carefully).

4. Based on the context of 4:1-6, explain if unity and peace are just a matter of attitude toward other people or just a matter of doctrinal soundness.

5. List and explain other **passages** that teach us the importance of unity and peace and how to achieve them.

6. What is the one body of 4:4? Prove your answer.

---

7. **Case Study:** List other **passages** showing that there is only one body in God's plan for our salvation. Explain what application this has to the denominational division of today.

Workbook on Ephesians and Philippians

8. What is the one Spirit of 4:4? (Note that the Father and the Son are also included in the list in 4:4-6. What does this show you about whether the Father, Son, and Holy Spirit are separate beings or the same individual?)

9. *Special Assignment:* List other **passages** that show that the Holy Spirit possesses the characteristics of a living spirit being, rather than just a power or force.

10. List other **passages** about the one hope. Explain what that one hope is.

11. List some examples of false hopes that may be taught by various religious groups.

12. Who is the one Lord – 4:5? List various ways in which His role or position is unique and no one else can serve in that role or position.

13. What is the one faith? Can we be pleasing to God if we believe there are many different faiths all of which are acceptable before Him? Explain your answer.

14. List some views that different people have about baptism. What are some different practices that different religious groups defend in regard to baptism?

15. *Special Assignment:* Explain and give proof for the gospel teaching about the one true baptism in each of the following ways:

* The action of baptism (sprinkling, pouring, or immersion)

* The purpose of baptism

* The candidate or subject of baptism (who should be baptized?)

16. Who is the one God and Father? How is He above all and through all and in all?

17. Explain the grace that has been given according to the measure of Christ's gift – 4:7.

18. What did Christ give to men when He ascended on high – 4:8-10? What does it mean that He led captivity captive?

19. Explain the sense in which Christ ascended, but first He descended.

20. According to 4:11, what are the gifts that Jesus gave to men when He ascended? (Think: Does the passage say that Jesus gave gifts to these different men or that the men themselves are the gifts? Explain your answer based on the context.)

21. ***Special Assignment: Define*** each of the different terms for the men that are listed in 4:11. List other ***passages*** for them and explain what work they do.

Apostles

Prophets

Evangelists

Pastors

Teachers

22. ***Case Study:*** Many denominations think that preachers are pastors. Explain and prove the difference between evangelists and pastors.

Workbook on Ephesians and Philippians

23. According to 4:12, what works are saints enabled to accomplish because of the roles filled by the men listed in 4:11?

24. **Define** keywords in 4:12 and explain how each applies to the work of the church.
Equip

Ministry

Edifying

25. According to 4:13,14, what purposes are accomplished by the works of verse 12?

26. **Special Assignment:** Some people think these verses are discussing spiritual gifts, saying that they will someday cease. Is that the point in this context? Are spiritual gifts, as such, being discussed in the context? Explain your answer.

27. How does unity of the faith and the knowledge of Christ fit the context of chapter 4? Explain how the gifts of verse 11 and the works of verse 12 bring about this unity.

28. Explain what it means to attain a perfect man, to the measure of the stature of the fullness of Christ. Explain how the gifts of verse 11 and the works of verse 12 bring this about.

29. According to 4:14, what is one reason why maturity is needed? List other **passages** about the dangers of false teachers.

30. According to 4:15, what should we do to help produce this maturity? Explain how such speaking helps lead to this maturity.

31. Explain why it is important that we speak the truth.

32. Explain why it is important that we speak in love.

33. Explain the illustration of 4:16 about the body. What role does this mean that we have as members of the body?

34. **Application**: In order for the body to achieve its goal, how many members must work? Should most of the work be left up to the leaders? What lessons should we learn?

35. Since most of the Ephesians were Gentiles, how does Paul describe the background from which they came – 4:17-19? (Think: How does this relate to the context of 2:12)?

36. **Define** the following terms from 4:19:
Lewdness

Uncleanness

Greediness

37. How did their background contrast to what Jesus taught – 4:20,21? What lessons should we learn for our lives?

38. Explain the concept of the old man versus the new man in 4:22-24. How is the old man described in contrast to the new man?

39. In order for this change to occur, what was to happen to the spirit of the mind – 4:23? Explain why the inner man is so important in this change.

40. What must we put away and what must we replace it with according to 4:25? What reason is given why we should do this?

41. **Application**: Give some examples of ways people can be guilty of falsehood. List some **passages** of Scripture about the importance of truth versus falsehood.

42. What must we put away according to 4:26? List **passages** about the dangers of anger. (Think: What does it mean to not let the sun go down on your anger?)

43. **Special Assignment:** Some people speak as though it is always sinful to be angry. Does the Bible contain examples of justifiable anger? Explain the danger that anger creates.

44. According to 4:27, how should we deal with the devil? Explain the meaning. (Think: How does this relate to the problem of anger and other temptations that we face?)

45. According to 4:28, what practice should we cease, and what should we do instead? List examples of ways people may be guilty of stealing.

46. List **passages** about the dangers of stealing.

47. **Application**: List **passages** about the importance of working to provide for our needs. What does it mean to work what is good? What applications does this have to gambling?

48. According to 4:29, what practice should we avoid, and what should we do instead? Explain the difference between that which is corrupt and that which is good.

49. List some ways we may be guilty of grieving the Holy Spirit – 4:30.

50. **Define** each of the following terms that describe things we should put away – 4:31:
Bitterness

Wrath, anger

Clamor

Railing

Malice

51. According to 4:32, what practices should replace what 4:31 said to put off?

52. **Define** kindness and tenderheartedness. Give examples that show how they will lead us to treat other people.

53. How should we forgive others according to 4:32? List other **passages** about forgiving others.

54. **Application**: Explain what it means to forgive others as God forgives us. List some specific principles this means we should follow in forgiving others.

Workbook on Ephesians and Philippians

Assignments on Ephesians 5

Please read the whole book of Ephesians again as we study chapter 5. Answer the following questions on chap. 5.

1. What should children of God do – 5:1? List some qualities of God that children of God should imitate.

2. What quality did Jesus demonstrate that we should imitate – 5:2? How did He demonstrate that quality?

3. What qualities are not fitting for saints according to 5:3? **Define** the terms.

4. **Application**: List examples of specific kinds of conduct that would fit the definition of fornication and therefore are not fitting for saints.

5. **Application**: List examples of specific kinds of conduct that fit the definition of covetousness and therefore should be avoided.

6. What kinds of conduct are not fitting for saints – 5:4? What should we do instead?

7. **Application**: Should verse 4 be used to prove that it is wrong for Christians to tell jokes or talk silly talk? Check various translations. Explain the proper application.

8. What will those who practice the sins of verse 3 not receive – 5:5,6? What will they receive instead?

9. Explain why Paul refers to covetousness as idolatry. What lessons should we learn?

10. Why do we need to be warned about deception regarding such matters? Describe some ways that people sometimes today try to deceive us to accept such conduct.

11. What reason does Paul give in 5:7,8 why we should not participate in the sins he has been discussing? Explain what it means to walk as children of light.

12. If we walk in light, not darkness, what will be the result in our lives – 5:9,10? How do we prove what is acceptable to the Lord?

13. What should we do and not do with these unfruitful works of darkness – 5:11?

14. *Application*: *Define* fellowship. List some ways that people sometimes are guilty of having fellowship with sin.

15. *Application*: List other passages about reproving or exposing evil. Is it enough for Christian simply to refuse to participate in sinful practices? Explain your answer.

16. Explain the sense in which it is shameful to speak of such practices – 5:12. Does this mean Christians should never even mention such practices or teach against them? (Note: Does Paul mention any such practices here?)

17. What is it that reproves or makes manifest what is right or wrong – 5:13? Explain the meaning and the application in context.

18. What other illustrations does Paul use in 5:14 to express our need to live as Christ wants us to? Where else are such illustrations used?

19. Considering all that Paul has said in the context, how should we walk – 5:15? Explain why wisdom is needed in order to walk properly.

20. Check various translations and explain what it means to redeem the time – 5:16. What reason is given why we should do so?

21. What must we do in order to be wise, not foolish – 5:17? List other **passages** showing that true wisdom comes from the word of God.

22. What sin is forbidden in 5:18? What should we do instead of this sin?

23. **Special Assignment**: Where the NKJV describes the consequence of drunkenness as "dissipation," what terms do other translations use? List other **passages** that describe the consequences of drinking alcoholic beverages.

24. List **passages** that instruct Christians to be sober or practice self-control. What application does this have to drinking alcohol? (Study also the terms used in 1 Peter 4:3.)

25. What act of worship is described in Ephesians 5:19? What kinds of songs should be used?

26. List other **passages** that show the kind of musical praise God has instructed us in the New Testament to use.

27. Discuss what we can learn about our worship from each of the following expressions used in the verse:

Speaking to one another

Singing

Making melody in your hearts to the Lord

28. **Application**: Do the terms in the verse emphasize the skill and talent of the singers or the message being conveyed in the words? What lessons and applications should we learn?

29. **Case Study:** Many churches use instrumental music in worship. Does an instrument do any of the things described in expressions in question number 27 above? Note: Where does the verse say we should make melody? Does any New Testament passage authorize the use of instruments in worship? What lessons should we learn and what conclusion should we reach?

30. What does 5:20 say we should do in praising God? List other **passages** about being thankful. (Think: To whom is this praise addressed and in whose name is it offered?)

31. **Define** submit. According to 5:21, who should submit to whom?

32. **Application**: Should all people submit to other people in the same sense? Explain the sense in which all Christians should submit to all others. What lessons should we learn?

33. How is the relationship of the husband and wife illustrated in 5:22-24? In what sense should wives submit to their husbands?

Workbook on Ephesians and Philippians

34. List other **passages** about the headship of the husband in the home and the wife's responsibility to submit.

35. Explain why authority is important when groups of humans work together. List other authority relationships that God has ordained.

36. Does the existence of authority mean that the one who possesses authority is more important than those who should submit? Explain the connection of Matthew 20:25-28.

37. **Case Study:** How does the teaching of the Scriptures compare to the concepts of modern feminism? How should we respond to the Women's Liberation movement?

38. From the comparison of Christ and the church to the relationship of husband and wife, what can we learn about how many true churches there are? What can we learn about how many heads the church may have?

39. What lessons should husbands learn from the relationship of Christ to the church – 5:25?

40. **Case Study:** Many people believe that the church is not essential to salvation. How important was the church to Jesus according to 5:23,25? What does this tell us about whether a person can be saved outside the church?

41. **Application**: List and explain some practical applications that husbands should learn from the fact that they should love their wives as Christ loved the church. Specifically, what lessons should husbands learn about how to use their authority properly?

42. What did Jesus do for the church – 5:26,27? *Define* some of the keywords used, such as sanctify, holy, without blemish, etc.

43. According to 5:26, how did Jesus cleanse the church? To what New Testament practice does the washing of water refer? List other *passages* about the importance of baptism.

44. What illustration is used to teach husbands to love their wives in 5:28-30?

45. How does a man treat his body which is similar to how he should treat his wife?

46. *Define* nourish and cherish. Explain lessons husbands should learn about how to treat their wives.

47. *Case Study:* Feminists and others often claim that Paul hated women or lacked respect for them. How would you respond based on the things Paul has taught husbands here?

48. What passage does Paul quote in 5:31? Summarize what the passage teaches about marriage, especially what it teaches about the relationship of husband and wife in our context.

49. According to 5:32, what subject is Paul primarily discussing in the overall context?

50. Nevertheless, what application does the passage have to husbands – 5:33? What application does it have to wives?

Workbook on Ephesians and Philippians

Assignments on Ephesians 6

Please read the whole book of Ephesians again as we study chapter 6. Answer the following questions on chap. 6.

1. What are children commanded to do in 6:1? Explain "in the Lord."

2. List other *passages* about the responsibilities of children to parents.

3. *Special Assignment:* Explain the advantages the child receives from submission to his parents. In particular, how does it help the child learn to relate to authority?

4. What else should children be taught in their responsibility to their parents – 6:2,3? List other *passages* about the responsibilities of children to honor their parents.

5. *Application:* List various ways that children sometimes fail to honor their parents.

6. What responsibility do fathers have to their children – 6:4? *Define* chastening and admonition.

7. List other *passages* about the responsibility of parents in raising children.

8. *Application*: List ways that parents sometimes provoke their children to wrath.

9. Describe some specific responsibilities that parents have in order to train their children in the Lord. That is, what is involved in fulfilling this responsibility? (Think: Why is this instruction addressed specifically to fathers?)

---

10. **Case Study:** Modern society advocates raising children permissibly with little or no authority. Others advocate other arrangements besides the natural parents raising children: homosexual marriage, government agencies, communes, etc. How should we respond based on this context and other passages?

---

11. What relationship is described beginning in 6:5? List other Bible **passages** about this relationship.

12. List and explain the principles that servants should follow in serving their masters according to 6:5-7.

13. Describe the ultimate reward of servants – 6:8.

14. Do these principles apply only to slaves, or also to hired servants? Explain.

15. What principles should masters follow in dealing with servants – 6:9? What is meant by doing the same things to them?

Workbook on Ephesians and Philippians

16. Ultimately, whom should masters seek to please? What lessons should they learn?

17. Study also Leviticus 25:39,47; Genesis 47:13-26; Exodus 21:5. Is the slave-master relationship, as described in Scripture, always as oppressive as often pictured today? Explain.

18. **Case study**: Some people believe that God intended to forbid slavery or to eventually eliminate it. Others claim that He simply restricted it to avoid abuses. Explain and prove which view is correct.

19. What has God provided to help us be strong in doing His work – 6:10,11? What are we able to do by the strength that God supplies?

20. **Define** wiles. Give some examples and explain how Satan uses wiles to defeat us.

21. **Application**: List other **passages** about the strength God can supply us. Explain the assurance this gives us that we can be victorious over sin and Satan. (See also verse 13.)

22. What information is given in 6:12 about the nature of our warfare? Give some examples of the powers and hosts of wickedness against which we struggle. What should we learn?

23. For each item of armor or part of the uniform described in 6:14-17, tell what God has provided and describe how it is important for our spiritual warfare.

Girdle for the waist

Breastplate

Feet shod

Shield

Helmet

Sword

24. What should accompany our use of the armor of God – 6:18? Explain why this practice is important in our warfare.

25. For what reason did Paul especially request their prayers – 6:19? Why is it important to pray for those who preach the gospel?

26. Whom had Paul sent to them, and how is he described – 6:21? For what purpose especially did Paul send him – 6:22?

27. In concluding, what blessings did Paul wish for the brethren to receive– 6:23,24?

Assignments on Philippians 1

Please read the whole book of Philippians at least once as we study chapter 1. Answer the following questions on chap. 1.

1. Who wrote this letter, and to whom is it addressed – 1:1?

2. List some things you know about Paul.

3. List some things you know about Timothy.

4. **Special Assignment:** Study a Bible dictionary or similar book about the city of Philippi. List some things you learned.

5. Make a list of Bible *passages* outside the book of Philippians that refer to the city or church at Philippi (use a concordance and cross-references).

6. Summarize what the Bible says about Philippi (the city or the church) outside the book of Philippians.

7. After you have read the whole epistle, state the theme of the book.

8. List some of the main points discussed in each chapter.

Extra Assignment: As you study the book, make a list of things the book says about joy and a list of things it says about support of gospel preachers.

9. List other *passages* about saints.

10. **Case Study:** Many people believe that saints are especially good Christians who died and have been appointed by a church so people can pray to them. How would you respond?

11. *Define* "bishop." List other *passages* about bishops.

12. *Case Study:* Some churches teach that bishops are a different office from elders. Others use "pastor" as just another name for a preacher. According to the Scriptures, what is the difference between bishops, elders, and pastors?

13. *Define* "deacons." List other *passages* about deacons and their work.

14. How did Paul express his view of the Philippians in 1:3,4?

15. For what in particular did he give thanks in 1:5? Explain what he meant.

16. What confidence did Paul express in 1:6? How does God work in the lives of His people? Conditionally or unconditionally? Explain.

17. How did the Philippians partake of Paul's work and blessings – 1:7? Explain.

18. List the things for which Paul prayed on behalf of the Philippians in 1:8-11.

19. Explain the connection between love, knowledge, and discernment. How do they relate to one another? Why should we abound in them?

20. What results would this love, knowledge, and discernment have in their lives if they applied them properly – 1:10,11? Why is it important to be sincere and without offense?

Workbook on Ephesians and Philippians

21. What are the fruits of righteousness? How much fruits of righteousness should we seek to have? What would the end result be?

22. Where was Paul at the time he wrote this (1:7,13-16)? How did he view the results of the troubles that he faced – 1:12?

23. Who had opportunity to learn as a result of Paul's circumstances – 1:13? (Think: How might this have happened?)

24. What effect had Paul's circumstances had on most brethren – 1:14? Is this what would normally be expected? Explain.

25. What good motives did some have for preaching – 1:15-17?

26. What bad motives did others have?

27. How did Paul view the preaching of the gospel, regardless of the motives of the preachers – 1:18? Would he have thought this way if these men were teaching error? Explain.

28. **Application**: Give examples that illustrate how people today sometimes preach truth but with bad motives. Does God approve of their bad motives? What lessons should we learn?

29. What did Paul expect to result from his circumstances – 1:19? What did he believe would bring about this result?

30. Was he certain whether he would live or die – 1:20? In either case, what did he expect and hope would be the most important outcome?

31. What advantage did Paul believe there would be if he continued to live – 1:21-24? Explain how this would be an advantage.

32. What advantage did he see if he were to die? Explain that advantage.

33. Did Paul prefer life or death? What does this tell you about Paul's faith and about his circumstances? (Think: Why might Paul be discussing this with the Philippians?)

34. What outcome did Paul have confidence would result from his circumstances – 1:25? How would this benefit the Philippians?

35. Did he hope to see them again – 1:26? What ultimate effect would this have?

36. Whether or not Paul saw them again, what kind of life did he urge them to lead – 1:27? What is required in order to live such a life?

37. How does he describe their need for unity? What can we learn from this about unity and what it takes to be united?

38. How should they view their adversaries – 1:28? What would be demonstrated about their enemies and about the Philippians?

39. What is expected of followers of Christ according to 1:29? List other **passages** about suffering for the cause of Christ.

40. **Special Assignment:** How did the Philippians' circumstances relate to those of Paul – 1:30? Explain how this may relate to the things he has discussed about his own circumstances throughout the chapter.

Assignments on Philippians 2

Try to read the whole book of Philippians again as we study chapter 2. Answer the following questions on chap. 2.

1. In what attitudes and blessings should we participate – 2:1? List and define each.

2. What should these attitudes and blessings produce in our lives – 2:2? Is unity just a matter of doctrinal correctness, or does it also require proper attitudes? Explain.

3. In order to have unity, what should not motivate our conduct – 2:3? How do these improper attitudes hinder unity in a congregation?

4. To have proper unity, how should we view others – 2:3,4? Explain how these attitudes will promote unity in a congregation.

5. Many translations of 2:3 say we should count others better than ourselves. Check other translations, and explain the meaning of this idea.

6. Where should we learn the proper attitude that Paul is encouraging – 2:5? Explain. (Note that verse 5 introduces the specific way that Jesus showed us an example in verses 6-8. These verses should be studied together as a unit.)

7. What position did Jesus have from eternity – 2:6? Compare "form of God" (2:6) with "form of a servant" (2:7). What can you learn about the meaning of "form" as used here?

8. **Special Assignment:** List other **passages** about the deity of Jesus. Did Jesus truly possess the nature of God? Explain and prove your answer.

9. Notice Hebrews 13:8. If Jesus possessed the nature of deity, could He lose that nature or the qualities that are essential to that nature? Did Jesus still possess deity on earth? Explain.

10. List various translations of the last part of 2:6. Explain the significance of grasping equality with God or thinking equality with God to be robbery as in these translations (note v7).

11. List various translations of the first part of 2:7. (Think: Once again, is it possible for deity to lose the characteristics or nature of deity?)

---

12. **Special Assignment:** Study the first part of 2:7 in light of the rest of verses 7,8. In what sense does the passage say that Jesus emptied Himself or made Himself of no reputation?

---

13. In what way did Jesus demonstrate humility according to 2:7,8? What lessons should we learn from this according to the context in 2:1-5?

14. List other **passages** about the humanity of Jesus. Was Jesus really a man on earth? Was He really God on earth?

15. What position has Jesus been given because of what He did – 2:9? Explain. (Think: How is the word "name" used in verses 9,10?)

16. What honor will men give Jesus for what He has done – 2:10,11?

17. What do we learn about salvation in 2:12? Explain fear and trembling.

18. List other **passages** that show that salvation requires us to work – that is, to obey. Does this mean we earn salvation? Explain.

Workbook on Ephesians and Philippians

19. Explain the significance of the fact we must work out our **own** salvation. List other **passages** showing that salvation is an individual responsibility.

20. In what sense does God work in us to will and to do His good pleasure – 2:13? Does this mean we have no choice about serving God? Explain.

21. How should we serve the Lord according to 2:14? What lessons should we learn?

22. What characteristics should children of God seek to develop– 2:15? Explain.

23. Why is it important for Christians to have such characteristics according to the passage? List other **passages** about our influence or example as Christians.

24. What role should the word of God have in our lives and example – 2:16? In what sense would their conduct affect Paul?

25. How did Paul view his service to them – 2:17,18? How was this a cause for joy?

26. What plans did Paul have for Timothy – 2:19? What was his purpose in this?

27. What praise did Paul give Timothy in 2:20?

28. What criticism did Paul raise of others in 2:21? What lessons should we learn?

29. How had Timothy demonstrated faithfulness – 2:22? How would the Philippians know this?

30. What hope did Paul express for the future – 2:23,24?

31. Describe the things we know about Epaphroditus according to the book of Philippians.

32. How does Paul describe Epaphroditus in 2:25? What should we learn about how to describe and address gospel preachers?

33. Explain the sense in which Epaphroditus was the messenger of the Philippians. List other related verses in the book of Philippians.

34. Why was Epaphroditus distressed – 2:26? How serious was his problem – 2:27?

35. What had God done for Epaphroditus? In what sense was this a blessing to Paul?

36. **Special Assignment:** List **passages** that explain the main purpose of miracles. Explain why Paul did not work a miracle to heal Epaphroditus.

37. Why was Paul sending Epaphroditus back to Philippi – 2:28?

38. How did Paul want the church in Philippi to treat Epaphroditus – 2:29?

39. What reason does Paul give why they should especially respect Epaphroditus – 2:30?

Assignments on Philippians 3

Try to read the whole book of Philippians again as we study chapter 3. Answer the following questions on chap. 3.

1. What is the source or ground of a Christian's joy – 3:1? Is our joy based primarily on our physical circumstances? Explain.

2. What reason does Paul give why he would write to them things they already knew? Explain the value of repetition in teaching.

3. What warning does Paul give in 3:2? Explain the terms that are used. What specific group of people would Paul be talking about (note the reference to circumcision in verse 3)?

4. Who does Paul say are the real circumcision – 3:3? List other **passages** showing the significance of being spiritually circumcised under the gospel.

5. What does it mean to have confidence in the flesh – 3:3 (note the context)? How does this apply to the people that Paul is discussing?

6. What claim does Paul make regarding confidence in the flesh – 3:4? What is his point?

7. What proofs does Paul give of his fleshly credentials – 3:5? Explain them.

8. How does he describe his zeal – 3:6? How did his conduct demonstrate his zeal?

9. What claim did he make about the law? What did this prove about his life as a Jew?

10. **Special Assignment:** What do verses 4-6 show about Paul's dedication to the Jewish religion? How would such facts affect his influence when he was converted?

11. After Paul was converted, how did he view the advantages he had as a Jew – 3:7?

12. What reason does he give in 3:8,9 why he was willing to suffer such losses? How did the things that he gave up compare to what he gained?

13. How was Paul made righteous – 3:9? List other similar **passages**.

14. **Case Study:** Some people use verse 9 to claim there is nothing we can do to be saved, but God must do everything to save us. Explain the sense in which we do not have our own righteousness but are made righteous by God. What did this have to do with the old law?

15. **Application**: Based on Paul's discussion, explain the lessons we should learn about our own willingness to sacrifice to serve God.

16. What goal did Paul pursue according to 3:10? What does it mean to know Jesus? How can we know the power of His resurrection?

17. How can we have fellowship in Jesus' sufferings and be conformed to His death?

18. What goal did Paul pursue according to 3:11? Since all will be raised, in what sense should we seek to attain to the resurrection?

19. What did Paul say that he had not yet achieved – 3:12,13? In what sense this was true?

20. **Application**: Explain the sense in which Paul forgot things behind and reached forward to things ahead. Give applications that show the importance of this principle to us.

Workbook on Ephesians and Philippians

21. Toward what did Paul press – 3:14? Explain what this goal or prize is.

22. What application should Paul's discussion have to us – 3:15,16? What will God do to help us in this, and how does He do it?

23. How should Paul's instructions affect our conduct and our thinking – verse 16?

24. How should Paul's example benefit us – 3:17? Who else should be a pattern for us?

25. **Case Study:** Some have denied that Biblical examples constitute binding authority. What do we learn from verse 17 about the importance of following examples? List other **passages** about following examples.

26. Whose example should we not follow – 3:18,19? How does Paul describe them? (Think: In what sense was their belly their God?)

27. In what sense do people set their mind on earthly things? List other similar **passages**. How does this help us understand whom Paul is discussing (compare verses 1-4)?

28. Where is our citizenship – 3:20? What does this teach about our priorities?

29. Who is already in heaven, and what do we anticipate that He will do – 3:21? List other similar **passages**.

30. What power does Jesus have? What does this show us about His character?

Assignments on Philippians 4

Try to read the whole book of Philippians again as we study chapter 4. Answer the following questions on chap. 4.

1. How did Paul describe the Philippians in 4:1? What did he urge them to do?

2. What two women did he address in 4:2? What did he urge them to do? What should we learn?

3. What had these women done, and what should others do for them – 4:3? What can we learn about women's role in working for the Lord?

4. List other **passages** about the Book of Life. Explain the significance of having one's name in the Book of Life.

5. What does Paul again admonish them to do in 4:4? List some reasons we have for rejoicing in the Lord.

6. 4:5 encourages us to practice "gentleness." What do other translations say instead of gentleness? What should we learn and how does this help us to have unity?

7. In what sense is the Lord at hand? What should we learn?

8. The KJV in 4:6 says to be careful for nothing. List alternate translations. Explain the meaning.

9. List other **passages** about anxieties and how to deal with worries.

Workbook on Ephesians and Philippians

10. *Application*: How are we taught to deal with our anxieties in 4:6? How would these practices help us when we are anxious? Explain specific applications we need to learn.

11. If we practice proper prayer and proper attitudes towards our anxieties, what will be the result – 4:7? How was Paul himself an example of this?

12. *Define* "meditate." List the things on which Paul says we should meditate and explain the meaning of each – 4:8?

13. *Application*: Explain why it matters what we focus our minds on. How can this help us in our choices, such as in entertainment, priorities, spirituality, courage, etc.?

14. How does the meditation that God's word advocates differ from the meditation of Hinduism, the New Age movement, and other Oriental religions?

15. What does Paul encourage the Philippians to practice in 4:9? What can we learn about teaching by example and about following New Testament examples? (See also 3:17.)

16. What joy did Paul express in 4:10?

17. **Define** "content." What did Paul say he learned in 4:11,12?

18. **Application**: Paul says this is a secret he learned. What are some things we need to learn in order to understand the secret? Is it always wrong to improve our circumstances?

19. What was the source of the strength Paul had – 4:13? What could he do as a result?

20. **Application**: What can we do through the strength Christ provides? Can Satan or people around us ever place temptations before us that are impossible to overcome? Explain.

21. How had the Philippians shared with Paul according to 4:14-16? When and where had they shared with Paul?

22. According to other passages, how had the Philippians' gift been conveyed to Paul? Did churches send funds to a central board of directors or the elders of another church who in turn oversaw the use and distribution of the funds?

23. According to 1 Peter 5:1-3; Acts 20:28; 14:23, what church should any specific eldership oversee? Does any New Testament passage authorize the elders of one church to oversee the work and funds of another church in evangelism?

24. Under what circumstances did churches send funds to another church? See Acts 11:27-30; Romans 15:25-27; 1 Corinthians 16:1-4; 2 Corinthians 8 and 9.

---

25. *Case Study:* In the sponsoring church arrangement, churches donate funds to be supervised by the elders of the sponsoring church, which is as financially capable of doing its own work as are the sending churches; but the sponsoring church has assumed ongoing oversight of a work that was as much the responsibility of the sending churches as it was of the sponsoring church. How would the passages we have studied apply to such a case?

---

26. What was especially important to Paul about the Philippians' gift – 4:17? In what way would this abound to the Philippians' account?

27. How had the Philippians' gift been sent to Paul – 4:18? Explain the expressions that he used to describe the gift.

28. What blessings did Paul believe God would give to the Philippians – 4:19? Compare 2 Corinthians 9:8-10.

29. Who receives the ultimate glory when God's people serve Him – 4:20? Explain.

30. What greetings does Paul send in 4:21-23? What is the significance of the reference to Caesar's household?

Made in the USA
Middletown, DE
14 July 2022